OUR LAST FAREWELL

CP/Robert Skinner

OUR LAST FAREWELL

PIERRE ELLIOTT
TRUDEAU

1919 - 2000

M&S

1919 · 2000

PIERRE ELLIOTT

Canadian Cataloguing in Publication Data

Main entry under title:
Our last farewell : Pierre Elliott Trudeau 1919-2000

ISBN 0-7710-8571-0

1. Trudeau, Pierre Elliott, 1919-2000 – Death and burial. 2. Trudeau, Pierre Elliott, 1919-2000 – Death and burial – Pictorial works. 3. Prime ministers – Canada – Death. 4. Prime ministers – Canada – Death – Pictorial works.

FC626.T7097 2000   971.064'4'092   C00-932637-5
F1034.3.T7097 2000

We acknowledge the financial support of the Government of Canada through the Book Publishing Industry Development Program for our publishing activities. We further acknowledge the support of the Canada Council for the Arts and the Ontario Arts Council for our publishing program.

Typeset in Minion by M&S, Toronto
Printed and bound in Canada

All photographs supplied by The Canadian Press.

McClelland & Stewart Ltd.
The Canadian Publishers
481 University Avenue
Toronto, Ontario
M5G 2E9
www.mcclelland.com

1   2   3   4   5   04   03   02   01   00

Above: Pavement artist Victor Fraser draws a 15-foot-long rose on Sunday, October 1, on a Toronto sidewalk.

Page 1: Philippe Brunelle, 6, of Pierrefonds, Quebec, sits behind a barricade in front of the Notre-Dame Basilica during the funeral in Montreal on Tuesday, September 3.

Opposite page: An RCMP honour guard escorts the hearse to Notre-Dame Basilica for the state funeral.

C O N T E N T S

"Justin and Sacha Trudeau

deeply regret to inform you

that their father, the Right Honourable

Pierre Elliott Trudeau,

passed away shortly after 3 p.m."

– Press release issued Thursday, September 28, 2000

In honour of
the Rt. Honourable
Pierre Elliot Trudeau

from the students
of
Laird School

CP/Fred Chartrand

Neighbours and admirers bring flowers, notes, and photographs to the door of Trudeau's residence in Montreal.

■ Page 6: A House of Commons worker lowers a flag on Parliament Hill on Thursday, September 28.

Mr. Trudeau was a great adversary. . . . He was a great intellectual, a brilliant orator and he defended with passion and intelligence his very deep convictions."

– Bloc Québécois leader Gilles Duceppe

CP/Jonathan Hayward

▲ The House of Commons observes a minute of silence on Friday, September 29.

▶ Clockwise from top left: The Leader of the Opposition, Alliance leader Stockwell Day, Bloc Québécois leader Gilles Duceppe, Conservative leader Joe Clark, and NDP leader Alexa McDonough followed Prime Minister Chrétien in commenting on Trudeau's passing.

It is ironic, sir, that a prime minister whose mobilizing purpose was the unity of his country should have so exacerbated the differences. . . . In a sense, he was too rational for this country, which after all was formed and grew against logic."

– Conservative leader Joe Clark

11

CP/Fred Chartrand

▲ On Friday, September 29, a single rose rests on a House of Commons desk.

▶ The funeral arrangements, announced on Friday, call for a state funeral. Trudeau's body is flown to Ottawa on Saturday morning. RCMP pallbearers carry it up the stairs to the Parliament Buildings on Saturday where it will take its place in the Hall of Honour for the weekend.

CP/Adrian Wyld

Margaret Trudeau, divorced from Pierre Trudeau in 1984, remained on good terms with him over the years. They shared in the upbringing of their three sons. The youngest, Michel, drowned after being swept into a lake by an avalanche in November 1998. On Saturday morning, September 30, Margaret arrives on Parliament Hill with her two surviving sons, Justin (centre) and Sacha.

CP/Jonathan Hayward

▲ Margaret Trudeau gives the Prime Minister a hug.

◄ Governor-General Adrienne Clarkson and her husband, John Ralston Saul, gather their thoughts in front of the casket. Waiting behind them are Prime Minister Jean Chrétien and his wife, Aline.

CP/Jonathan Hayward

▲ Parliamentarians and dignitaries pay their respects to the former prime minister.

▶ A mourner touches the casket.

"It's one of those times you feel you just have to be here,
to share with other people."
– Catherine Casserly, Ottawa resident

CP/Jonathan Hayward

▲ The line curls around the lawns on Parliament Hill.

◀ Mourners inch their way through an arch on Parliament Hill waiting their turn to pay their respects to the former prime minister.

CP/Jonathan Hayward

The press might have led it to a certain extent, but I truly believe this outpouring would have happened anyhow. The public grieving is unlike anything we've seen in our lifetime."

– Jack Granatstein, historian

▲ As the lines begin to form on Parliament Hill, it becomes apparent that the public turnout for the lying-in-state will surpass any comparable occasion in modern Canadian history. Trudy Holmes (left), wearing Trudeau election campaign buttons, breaks into tears as she waits to pay her respects. Ottawa resident Althea Ford (right) is part of the crowd on Parliament Hill.

◄ The view from across the street on Sunday.

CP/Jonathan Hayward

▲ Neil Trifunovich stops to look at a window display in memory of the former prime minister in downtown Ottawa.

◄ Mourners leave messages and roses at the Centennial Flame on Sunday evening.

■ Previous pages: Temporary fences guide mourners to the Centre Block. Authorities estimated that visitors passed through the hall at a rate of between 1,000 and 1,600 an hour.

THE JOURNEY HOME

"I consider him a man of the people.

He spoke his mind

and from the heart and

I think that's very hard to find today."

– Mario Nascimento, VIA service manager

CP/Jonathan Hayward

▲ RCMP pallbearers carry the casket under the arches of the Peace Tower on Monday, October 2.

◄ Sacha (left) and Justin Trudeau watch as the casket is loaded into the hearse.

■ Page 28: Margaret Trudeau hugs her eleven-year-old daughter, Alicia Kemper, as they watch the casket leave the Hall of Honour.

We are bringing Mr. Trudeau home. Montreal was the place of his birth, the place where he spent most of his life, the place where he retired when he left politics. It's where ~~he~~ died and the place where he will be buried."

– Marc Lalonde, friend and political colleague

CP/Adrian Wyld

CP/Andrew Vaughan

▲ Mourners wave as the funeral train – Special Train No. 638 – passes through the Eastern Ontario town of Limoges, 30 kilometres from Ottawa.

◄ The train passed people in business suits standing in parking lots, workers outside factories, flag-waving schoolchildren. Some wept, others reached out to touch the rail cars. Some doffed their caps or held their hands over their hearts.

CP /Toronto Star/Rick Madonik

▲ A large crowd gathers around the train carrying Pierre Elliot Trudeau as it passes through Alexandria, Ontario.

▶ Justin Trudeau accepts flowers, a flag, and a heart-shaped balloon when the train stops briefly in Alexandria.

▲ Mourners turn out to greet the funeral train at the Dorval, Quebec, train station.

▶ A mourner reaches out to pass a rose to Justin (top) and Sacha Trudeau at the Dorval station.

CP/André Forget

▲ Mourners file into Montreal City Hall to pay their respects to Trudeau. Earlier, onlookers had erupted into a heartfelt rendition of "O Canada" when Justin and Sacha entered the building.

◄ Children across Canada joined in the mourning, each in their own way. Four-year-old Christopher Buckle (previous pages) holds a rose which he brought to a memorial mass at St. Michael's Church, Toronto. Melissa Lowe, 7 (opposite page), stands on a chair to sign a message to Pierre Trudeau, together with her sister, Amanda, 14, at the Alberta Legislature in Edmonton.

▲ As in Ottawa, visiting hours were extended to accommodate public demand. The doors of Montreal City Hall were closed at 11:00 p.m. on Monday night.

◀ Quebec Premier Lucien Bouchard stands before the casket during the lying-in-state ceremony at Montreal's City Hall.

STATE FUNERAL

"In all his legendary freedom of style
and thought, in the midst of storms and
upheavals, he remained faithful to what
he held most dear: his family,
his friends, his country, and his faith."

– The Reverend Jean-Guy Dubuc

CP/Andrew Vaughan

▲ Mourners standing in front of the Notre-Dame Basilica reveal the depth of their emotions during the funeral.

▶ Margaret Trudeau sits between her sons, Sacha (top) and Justin at the Notre-Dame Basilica. Among the dignitaries to attend the funeral are Cuban president Fidel Castro, former U.S president Jimmy Carter, Britain's Prince Andrew, actor Margot Kidder, and the poet Leonard Cohen. Three former Canadian prime ministers are in attendance: John Turner, Joe Clark, and Brian Mulroney.

■ Page 44: Mourners outside the basilica watch as the casket is carried inside.

EULOGY BY ROY HEENAN

Family friend and business partner

CP/Paul Chiasson

My colleague Jacques Hébert will address you in French.

He or myself could render homage to Pierre Elliott Trudeau in both English or French and we would be understood by a majority of Canadians.

Like most Canadians I admired the prime minister – Pierre Elliott Trudeau. Our political leaders have eloquently testified of him as a leader and as a public man.

But I would like to talk to you about the private person who lived amongst us for the last 15 years. We came to know him as a warm and compassionate man invariably courteous to anyone he met. He was unassuming. He walked to work. He cared not for the trappings of power. One could not walk among the streets beside him without being stopped by somebody who wanted to shake his hand or say a few words to him. He was invariably cordial, patient and polite.

I have also learned the warmth of his friendship and I witnessed the depth of the love for his children. Justin, Sasha, Sarah – your father loved you and Mishu so very much. He was devoted to you. He was so proud of you. No one could ever go into his office or talk to him for a few minutes without realizing that you were never far from his thoughts.

The world knows that you have suffered a terrible loss but you will bear it secure in the certain knowledge of his great love for you. That must be your strength.

It has been said that Pierre Trudeau was aloof and distant. That is not the Pierre Trudeau I knew. On the contrary he was caring, polite and kind, and he had such judgement. It was a privilege to discuss with him matters of the moment and witness his acute and analytical mind ready to engage in any discussion with enormous civility.

I will also remember the vigorous man who loved the outdoors. He loved skiing. His skiing style can only be described as daredevil. But he was afraid of no mountain and he delighted in the challenge. It was with great regret that he told me last April that this winter was the first winter in 75 years that he had not skied and he was sad.

He loved the oceans, swimming and scuba diving and of course canoeing. He wrote that the art of governing had some parallels with the art of canoeing. Sometimes you have to fight against the current. He never hesitated to do that.

I'm told that Pierre Elliott Trudeau died last Thursday. The man maybe, but his ideas live on. I speak not as a politician but as an ordinary citizen.

◀ Sacha Trudeau delivers a reading from the book of Daniel as part of the funeral service.

Over the last few days, citizens by the tens of thousands have turned out to bear witness of their love and admiration for Pierre.

We saw it in Ottawa on Parliament Hill. We saw it on the train that brought him back home to his beloved city. And we saw it again here in Montreal in the last two days.

And why? Why do the citizens respond so spontaneously? Because he was a remarkable leader? That's true, but it's not because of that. It is because he created and articulated a vision of this country which resonates in the hearts and minds of millions of Canadians. He defended that vision both rationally and passionately both at home and abroad.

And what is that vision that is shared by so many? First, of peoples living together in harmony in a single state and that brother not be turned against brother. Second, that we aspire to a just society, one that offers equality of opportunity. A vision of understanding of and charity towards others, particularly the less fortunate. That the two cultures of Canada flourish and be nurtured across this great land. And that other cultures enrich us. That bilingualism is an asset, not a liability. And, of course, that the fundamental rights and freedoms be ensured and enshrined for all Canadians.

This vision has changed forever the sense of ourselves as a society.

This is his legacy to us. This is the testament of Pierre Elliott Trudeau, who left it to all Canadian men and women that he loved so well.

We will also remember that on a deeper and more personal level he challenged us all to be the very best that we could be.

We have been touched by greatness. Today we say au revoir to Pierre and we bury the body. But the vision continues. The vision lives.

EULOGY BY JACQUES HÉBERT*

Former senator and longtime friend

CP/Paul Chiasson

Pierre Trudeau was very fond of this saying by Aristotle: "The main goal of society is to allow its members to live *full lives*, both collectively and individually."

And throughout his years at the head of the government, he pursued that goal with his distinctive resolve. He was convinced that helping youth find fulfilment was a priority. Over the last few days, much has been said about his most spectacular accomplishments: the constitution, the Charter of Rights and Freedoms, official languages, etc. But did anyone mention his immense compassion for the youth of this country? He for one never hesitated to place youth programs among his finest accomplishments . . . programs such as the unique and daring Opportunities for Youth, and, if I dare say, Canada World Youth and Katimavik . . . which he still fondly mentioned to me some ten days before his death . . . In a voice barely audible, as though it were already from another world.

Hundreds of thousands of young people have changed profoundly, enjoying "full" and productive lives thanks to one of Pierre Trudeau's youth initiatives. Before he came along, youth had been a voiceless minority and of little interest to politicians.

One day in 1959, if memory serves, way before his sensational entry into politics, I'd asked him to help me pull a young orphan from the clutches of the rotten system in place at the time. It so happened that this was an "illegitimate" orphan, as they were then known. (A "Duplessis orphan," in today's parlance.) Donning his lawyer's gown – something he rarely did – Pierre Trudeau threw himself heart and soul into a battle that lasted several months until the 19-year-old victim was able to recover his freedom and dignity.

One of the countless examples of Pierre Trudeau's generosity.

He was young and free at the time, though dunces called him a playboy because he was sometimes spotted on a ski hill, or even in a discotheque! On Saturdays perhaps. But the rest of the week – his friends can confirm it – he'd labour away writing articles, essays and briefs that would foster the Quiet Revolution and disrupt established ideas. He was one of the most passionate (and scarce) defenders of Quebec's fledgling and barely tolerated labour movement, and of our ceaselessly flouted civil liberties.

To his admirers, Pierre Trudeau remains a hero and giant. A kind of superman, a proud and courageous knight from another era, a man of immense and disconcerting culture, one of unusual intelligence serving Quebec and Canada, a province and country he loved passionately. But

---

* Translated by Jean-Paul Murray

whoever had the privilege of being his friend remembers a Pierre Trudeau very different from the electrifying, unpredictable and extraordinary figure the media doted on, as though bewitched!

To his friends, Pierre Trudeau was primarily a happy companion, a human being of rare simplicity and infinite sensitivity, very thoughtful, and loving even – something that ought to astonish the ignorant gossip scribblers who dared speak of his arrogance.

He had an exquisite sense of friendship: that's why the illness and death of his friend Gérard Pelletier, our mutual friend, marked him so deeply. After the funeral, with a sigh, he whispered these rather incredible words from such a circumspect man: "I've just lost a part of my soul!"

The day we learned of Pierre Trudeau's death, though it was expected, many of us experienced the same anguish: part of ourselves had just departed forever!

Whether as friends or political foes, he profoundly marked us all by forcing us to think, to question ourselves and debate ideas rather than feelings. Because of Pierre Trudeau, we have become better human beings, and Canada is now a more generous and caring country. As he once said: "A country can be influential in the world by the size of its heart and the breadth of its mind, and this is the role Canada can play."

Among Pierre Trudeau's qualities, there is at least one on which everyone agrees: he was an admirable father until he drew his last breath, and totally devoted to his children, though he could have allowed himself to be distracted or overcome by the exacting demands of his prime ministry.

He adored his three sons and daughter, and, with infinite patience, bequeathed his fundamental values to them, his love of culture and nature, his sense of discipline. When I think of Pierre Trudeau, I can only see him surrounded by his three boys, at different times in their lives, as in the numerous photos and portraits that graced the walls of his office.

We can all delight in one thing at least: he died in peace, lucid, serene, resigned, happy, surrounded by Justin, Sacha and Margaret.

Oh! How he deserved this last moment of grace!

It may not be fitting, inside such a noble church, to close this kind of speech with words from a . . . miscreant! But Pierre Trudeau was extremely fond of Charles Baudelaire and all true poets!

Happy is he who with a sprightly wing
Can fly to bright and peaceful meadows;

Whose thoughts, like larks
Rise freely in the morning sky,
Hovering over life, readily conversant with
The language of flowers and muted things.

So long old friend! Rest well . . . while we continue to love you!

EULOGY BY JUSTIN TRUDEAU

CP/Paul Chiasson

Friends, Romans, countrymen.

I was about six years old when I went on my first official trip. I was going with my father and my Grandpa Sinclair up to the North Pole.

It was a very glamorous destination. But the best thing about it is that I was going to be spending lots of time with my dad because in Ottawa he just worked so hard.

One day, we were in Alert, Canada's northernmost point, a scientific military installation that seemed to consist entirely of low shed-like buildings and warehouses.

Let's be honest. I was six. There were no brothers around to play with and I was getting a little bored because Dad still somehow had a lot of work to do.

I remember a frozen, windswept Arctic afternoon when I was bundled up into a Jeep and hustled out on a special top-secret mission. I figured I was finally going to be let in on the reason of this high-security Arctic base.

I was exactly right.

We drove slowly through and past the buildings, all of them very grey and windy. We rounded a corner and came upon a red one. We stopped. I got out of the Jeep and started to crunch across towards the front door. I was told, no, to the window.

So I clambered over the snowbank, was boosted up to the window, rubbed my sleeve against the frosty glass to see inside and as my eyes adjusted to the gloom, I saw a figure, hunched over one of many worktables that seemed very cluttered. He was wearing a red suit with that furry white trim.

And that's when I understood just how powerful and wonderful my father was.

Pierre Elliott Trudeau. The very words convey so many things to so many people. Statesman, intellectual, professor, adversary, outdoorsman, lawyer, journalist, author, prime minister.

But more than anything, to me, he was Dad.

And what a dad. He loved us with the passion and the devotion that encompassed his life. He taught us to believe in ourselves, to stand up for ourselves, to know ourselves and to accept responsibility for ourselves.

We knew we were the luckiest kids in the world. And we had done nothing to actually deserve it.

It was instead something that we would have to spend the rest of our lives to work very hard to live up to.

He gave us a lot of tools. We were taught to take nothing for granted. He doted on us but didn't indulge.

Many people say he didn't suffer fools gladly, but I'll have you know he had infinite patience with us.

He encouraged us to push ourselves, to test limits, to challenge anyone and anything.

There were certain basic principles that could never be compromised.

As I guess it is for most kids, in Grade 3, it was always a real treat to visit my dad at work.

As on previous visits, this particular occasion included a lunch at the parliamentary restaurant, which always seemed to be terribly important and full of serious people that I didn't recognize.

But at eight, I was becoming politically aware. And I recognized one whom I knew to be one of my father's chief rivals.

Thinking of pleasing my father, I told a joke about him – a generic, silly little grade school thing.

My father looked at me sternly with that look I would learn to know so well, and said: Justin, never attack the individual. One can be in total disagreement with someone without denigrating him as a consequence.

Saying that, he stood up and took me by the hand and brought me over to introduce me to this man. He was a nice man who was eating with his daughter, a nice-looking blond girl a little younger than I was.

My father's adversary spoke to me in a friendly manner and it was then that I understood that having different opinions from those of another person in no way precluded holding this person in the highest respect.

Because mere tolerance is not enough: we must have true and deep respect for every human being, regardless of his beliefs, his origins and his values. That is what my father demanded of his sons and that is what he demanded of our country. He demanded it out of love – love of his sons, love of his country.

That is why we love him so. These letters, these flowers, the dignity of the crowds who came to say farewell – all of that is a way of thanking him for having loved us so much.

My father's fundamental belief never came from a textbook. It stemmed from his deep love for and faith in all Canadians and over the past few days, with every card, every rose, every tear, every wave and every pirouette, you returned his love.

It means the world to Sacha and me.

Thank you.

We have gathered from coast to coast to coast, from one ocean to the other, united in our grief, to say goodbye.

But this is not the end. He left politics in '84. But he came back for Meech. He came back for Charlottetown. He came back to remind us of who we are and what we're all capable of.

But he won't be coming back anymore. It's all up to us, all of us, now.

The woods are lovely, dark and deep. He has kept his promises and earned his sleep.

Je t'aime, papa.

▶ Margaret Trudeau listens raptly to Justin's address.

CP/Paul Chiasson

▲ Only after he had delivered his eulogy did Justin Trudeau briefly lose his composure and rest his head on the flag-draped casket.

▶ Clockwise from left: Justin, Margaret, and Sacha Trudeau, Deborah Coyne, Roméo Leblanc, and Cuban president Fidel Castro watch as Cardinal Turcotte blesses the casket.

He was the most interesting man of our times. . . .
The music died when he retired. Politics was never the same."

– Peter Bregg, news photographer

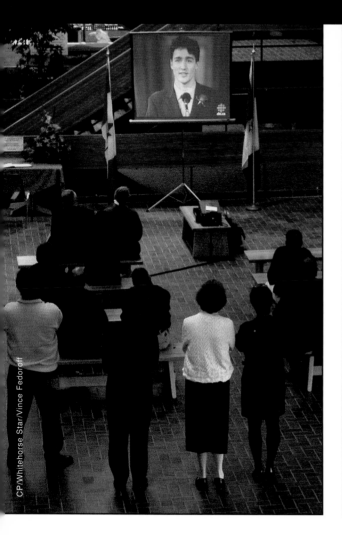

▲ Across the country – from a government building in Whitehorse to a barber shop in Saint John – people paused to take in the funeral service.

▶ The casket is carried out of Notre-Dame Basilica at the conclusion of the funeral service.

> "The applause, the anthem – it was very hard not to cry. We felt very privileged and very proud to be walking beside Mr. Trudeau's hearse. I thought of him the whole way."
>
> – Const. Sylvain L'Heureux, a member of the RCMP detail assigned to slow march beside the hearse

CP/André Forget

CP/Andrew Vaughan

▲ Nine-year-old Sarah Coyne, daughter of Pierre Trudeau, wipes her eye as she watches her father's casket being loaded into the hearse.

◄ Outside the Basilica, a hearse waits to take the body of the former prime minister to the family crypt in St-Rémi-De-Napierville.

▲ Prime Minister Jean Chrétien waves goodbye while his wife, Aline, blows a kiss as the hearse pulls away from the Basilica.

▶ Justin Trudeau, carries the rose which, in an impulsive gesture, he later gives to a young girl standing among the mourners outside of the Basilica.

A man places a homemade flag as a tribute to the former prime minister at the Trudeau family crypt in St-Rémi-De-Napierville on the south shore of Montreal, on Wednesday, October 4, 2000. Trudeau was buried there in a brief, private ceremony after the state funeral on Tuesday.